My Channeled Energy

My Channeled Energy
A collection of poems and short stories

Jennifer D. Vassel

BuddingRose Publications
www.BuddingRosePublications.com

My Channeled Energy: A collection of poems and short stories

By Jennifer D. Vassel

Copyright © 2014 Jennifer D. Vassel

All rights reserved. Except as permitted under the US Copyright Act of 1976, no part of this publication may be reproduced, distributed, or transmitted in any form or by any means or stored in a database or retrieval system, without the prior written permission of the publisher.

BuddingRose Publications
www.BuddingRosePublications.com

Cover Illustration by Brette Sims
Cover Design by Reiko Gordon

Printed in the United States of America

ISBN 10: 0991555600
ISBN 13: 978-0-9915556-0-4 (pbk)
ISBN 978-0-9915556-1-1 (ebook)

This book is for all those who put actions behind their words. Those who said they were going to do something and went through all measures to get. It. Done. Be proud of yourself—you let your inner you bloom.

Acknowledgments

First and foremost, I give thanks to God for blessing me with the opportunity to accomplish another life goal. This book could not have been completed without the steadfast love, support, and encouragement from my family and friends. Thank you all for being there for me during this journey.

A Message from the Author

In his "Year of Intention" sermon, Bishop Dale C. Bronner said, "Don't die with your gifts still inside of you; impart to others what was entrusted to you." Talk about the power of words and how they can move you to *act*. I was called to action when I listened to his message on the eve of 2013. Since then, my perception of life has changed; it has been filled with intent and purpose.

My Channeled Energy is a compilation of poems and short stories written over the span of twenty years. Some were homework assignments, while others were for leisure. Either way, I used the writing opportunity so my thoughts could take on written transformation.

If you know me personally, you know that I'm a very private person, but I had to ask myself one day, "What good is devoting twenty years of creative expression if only a select few have experienced it?" That said, I am opening my "book" to you, and I invite you to come along for the journey.

Walt Disney said it best: "The way to get started is to quit talking, and begin doing." I have been entertaining the idea of going public with my work for quite some time now. Just as how I was moved to act, I wish you all the same experience. If this book serves as a catalyst leading to inspiration, enlightenment, transformation, or all of the above, then it has served its purpose.

Happy reading,
Jennifer

My Channeled Energy (Theme Poem)

Like a spiritual conduit from mind to pen,

my channeled energy flows so freely.

The shadows that were once tightly caged within

are finally loosed and letting me be.

Such a liberating feeling I'm blessed to feel—

although hidden reservations do dangle.

But after deep contemplation, I must reveal

the birth of written art when thoughts untangle.

Contents

Acknowledgments i

A Message from the Author ii

My Channeled Energy (Theme Poem) iii

Poems

Elementary & Junior High School

    Rainbow Birds 1

    Black Beauty 2

    I Am Cowardly, Yet Brave 3

    It 4

    Mother's Day 5

High School

    A New Beginning 9

    Burning 10

    Emotions 11

    Flawless Imperfection 12

    Sacrifices 14

    There Is Something Missing 15

    Tired 16

    Waiting 17

College

Dear Love Critic 21
Listen 23
Misunderstood 24
Scar(RED) 26
Sealed with a Kiss (A Cento*) 27
White Wave 29
Write Me a Poem 30

Beyond

180° 33
Actionnairess 35
Anxiety 36
A User's Guide 37
Book in Me 38
Change 39
Clarity 40
Deceit 41
Detached 42
Dreams 43
Empath 44
Four Elements 45
Hen Pen 47
Hot Yoga 49

Human Hamster 50
In a Moment in Time 51
Intellectual Stimulation 52
Lost 53
Masseuse 54
Metamorphosis 55
No Other 56
Post Grad Bluez 57
Purging 58
Rain 59
Seclusive Destruction 60
Stallion 61
The Budding Rose 63
The Storm 64
To My Son Not Yet Conceived 65
Trapped Until Freed 66
Truth 67
Vicarious Girl 68
Voice 69
Who Am I? (A Lady's Anthem) 70

Short Stories

A Man of Few Words 75
A MINDful Testimony 78
A MINDful Testimony—The Aftermath 80

Stage Five 81
The Race for Success.. 83
Taking a Leap of Faith.. 84
The Power of Patience and Prayer 89

From Me to You 92
Appendix.. 93

Poems

Elementary & Junior High School

Rainbow Birds

Rainbow birds flutter by,

They fly so high in the sky.

They make me dance, they make me sing,

They make me do anything.

I love the rainbow birds,

They speak in many different words.

Now I have to go—

But no need to shout!

Rainbow birds are all about.

Black Beauty

Black Beauty is a wonderful horse

Her hair is silky, not coarse

Her eyes are hazel brown

Black Beauty never frowns

She likes to smell flowers

And take showers for long hours

She glitters like snowflakes

She likes to eat cupcakes

Black Beauty wants to be friends with you and me,

And that's the way it ought to be

I Am Cowardly, Yet Brave

I am cowardly, yet brave.
I wander aimlessly through life's obstacles, not knowing what
    is set forth beyond me.
I hear the calls of memories, begging to be remembered,
    waiting to be found.
I want to live a long life—not too short, not too long.
I am cowardly, yet brave.

I pretend to feel good, yet inside I am burning with pain.
I feel the warmth of one's smile, as my smile slowly appears.
I touch the hands of others to reveal a soft grin.
I worry about things that make my palms sweat, and shivers
    crawl down my spine.
I cry when others hurt me and judge who I am.
I am cowardly, yet brave.

I understand the feelings and secrets others share with me.
I say things to make people feel good.
I dream of one day being the most respected person, and at
    the same time, one who is truthful and honest.
I hope my life will be full of wonderful experiences.
I am cowardly, yet brave.

It

And there it laid

So quiet

Motionless

Ready to grab me and bring me down with it

I stood there

Feeling the sweat trickle down my face

Listening to my heart thump—

Buh-bum, buh-bum, buh-bum

The room—so dark, filling the air with screaming silence

Suddenly, I see it

Under my bed…

A little thing staring at me

Giggling, laughing hysterically,

Making me feel like an idiot

Now I wonder, was I like that at six?

Mother's Day

Today is Mother's Day, Mother's Day, indeed

When all the children bring gifts, as their mothers need

From books to toys, or a cute little doll,

Or maybe even a shopping spree at the mall

A mother is gracious, a mother is kind,

A mother is all the cool things you can find

So, let's clap our hands and give a cheer

For all the mothers who are both far and near

High School

A New Beginning

My heart resurfaced,

Escaped from inner darkness—

Light can now be seen.

Burning

The fury in my heart burns inside of me
Hotter than the deepest depths of hell
This is not the way I want to be
But, there's no one I can tell

The sting of water from my eyes
Is how my emotions show
But, if there's one thing I could advise,
Don't let anyone know

I want people to like me for me,
Not some trophy on the wall
I'm suffocated by what I'm "supposed" to be
That I don't know who I am at all

The fury in my heart burns inside of me,
If anyone can see
I'm scraping my remains off the floor
'Cause I don't want to live like this anymore

Emotions

Gazing into the depths of the sea, I face him

His eyes, browner than rich soil,

Viewing me, scanning me,

Reaching my heart in impossible ways

Silence

Screaming to be heard

I could not speak

I could not breathe

His hand on my face,

Caressing me, coaxing me

My heart pounding vigorously

We lean closer, our eyes still hooked

His hands

Hugging my waist

Our eyes come to darkness,

And I feel them,

His lips, so soft,

Luring me into his soul

Flawless Imperfection

I am alone in darkness, where silence surrounds me,
Sparing innocent eyes from my internal reality
Comparing my thoughts to unreal things,
I am engulfed in my own misery

My mirror's reflection lies to me,
Drowning in pain; pain that no one can see
Flipping through pages of my fantasies—
A monster is hidden within

Just listen; listen to my cries
All I want is to be found
I give in to temptation, possessing power to fulfill my dreams,
But it's overwhelming

I lie on my bed…thinking, wishing, dreaming, watching
      emptiness pour from my walls
No one knows, except the very depths of my soul
It feels good to break the boundaries,
But it's quickly replaced with the rush of over-powering shame

Tears stream down my bitter face
The monster within cannot be exposed
So, I am punished again and again and again

No one seems to care that I'm dying inside
My flawless imperfection deceives them
The mirror reflects this shallow world, where
I am falling, waiting for someone to catch me,
Except no one does.

Failure. I am alone again.

Sacrifices

Take, O take priceless possessions away

They so sweetly wander alone

And quietly whisper a song of sorrow

People they see feel their pain,

But their hearts shatter coldly, shatter coldly

Loss of direction, but run along boldly; run along boldly

There is Something Missing

The hardest thing in the world is to stay silent,
Straddling down words and feelings, getting ready to explode
    out of me,
Shrinking me down to nothing.
Anger burns inside of me;
I can breathe, yet I am suffocating.
I speak, yet no one hears.
I have kept it in,
Putting on a fake face,
Drowning in darkness while still appearing as though
    everything's all right
To the point where I want to cry,
Except the tears won't fall;
There is something missing.

Tired

I am tired

Of running

Of running away from my fears

Of keeping things to myself

Of not letting anyone know the real me

Of not being able to tell people what's going on in my life

Things are running in and out of my mind

But I can't tell anyone

It is hard to explain

I am tired

I have so much to think about

So much to decipher

So much to solve

To sit and wonder about

My heart is forever being hurt

If you were to open it up, it would be filled with cuts

Filled with bruises

Filled with scrapes

Bandages and stitches

I am filled with pain

I am tired

Waiting

To wait in a never-ending line

I cannot express enough how unbearable it is…

Yet, it is what I live for

To get that sense of belonging,

To be held in his arms and feel the warmth of his soul,

To just get lost in his eyes…

It is what I yearn for

To kiss his soft lips and be lifted off my feet with his tantalizing scent,

To just be in…

Yeah, that's what I wait for

College

Dear Love Critic

Dear Love Critic,

It's funny how you try to come around me with your open
      legs and closed mind, trying to define what I call my love.

When you let them turn that easy knob
      to your wide open door

So they can come, and leave, and then shut you out,

But then you wanna talk about my love?

Dear Love Critic,

You think that flaunting the quantity of testosterone you talk
      to is something cute?

Whoever heard of a Barbie doll with ten different Kens?

Tossed around by filthy hands, used and reused 'til they're
      tired of playing

You're just a game, a game of chess, where you should check
      your mate's real intentions—

You're nothing but a shed for them to cram their rusty tools in.

Dear Love Critic,

Now I see the negativity that comes out your lips is 'cause
      what goes through your lips is heartless

Each stroke strangling, suppressing, take, take, taking away
      'til you're broke of your own dignity.

And, it seems to me this jealousy is how you cope with it

This love, or lack thereof, the loveless like of a love critic.

So, Dear Love Critic—you should get a new hobby.

Listen

Warm touch

Gentle sounds

Fist against muscle and bone

Listen.

Sensuous

is the conversation between lips and neck

to the finger tips and body

They're whispering—

Listen.

His heart's windows open as it beats

slowly

The blinds are open, and now I see

What lies and is hidden deep within...*shhhhhhh*

Just listen.

Misunderstood

Stare deep into my eyes, and you will see
The carnivorous beast which lies within me,
Swift as a snake that sneaks through the sand,
Yet falls weak to a gentle hand.

Its rhythmic motion up and down my spine;
I'm the best companion you'll ever find.
I'm self-maintained and low-maintenance, you see,
No need to throw senseless Frisbees at me.

Dismiss the superstitions of my friendship with the devil
Because I am not evil on any level.
All the negativity made against me you hear
Was connivingly plotted 'cause the "man's best friend" does fear.

My sound is like poetry, comforting to the soul,
While his vulgar noise annoys—yes, that is his goal.
Keep on running around chasing your tail!
We are the creatures that will prevail.

Felis catus is my scientific name,
And educating the uneducated is my game.
I make you sneeze, your nose, and eyes run?
Oh, please, that could be caused by anyone.
Loving, soothing, caring, and true:

These are the qualities we can offer to you.

Now, after hearing my case, if you would

Please understand why we are so misunderstood.

Scar(RED)

A white dress stained red

shields her skin's tears

as the red tie ties around a heart so deadly,

so deadly that it stenches the air and bleeds through the red sheets.

Her skin's tears

sing a red song,

while in a white dress stained red.

The rage in red eyes

glimpses a glass bottle filled with red temptation

and a red rose attached to a love letter sealed with scars.

Sealed With a Kiss (A Cento*)

Pale love lost in a thaw of fear

Overtakes me,

Guarded by a glittering tear

For the tears that drip all over

A willow deeply scarred

And built on tragedies

Grows higher than the soul can hope or mind can hide

I claim [thee] utterly in a kiss—

Come, for thy kiss was warm,

[While] I sit by the fire and hear

The echo of an ancient speech

Gnawing at my sanity

A kiss…

Earth has not anything to show more fair,

More lovely and more temperate,

I say aloud

The eyes of heaven shine

Upon the breathless starlit air

Skin, muscle, hair, eyes, larynx, we

Wonder what will be

Never mind silent fields

The sessions of sweet silent thought:

[Just] take this kiss upon a brow,

And let me love.

Sources for this cento can be found in the Appendix

White Wave

Mysteriousness…

Listen to the quiet shores;

Its depth is profound.

Write Me a Poem

I want you to write me a poem

I'm not talking about a "Roses are red, violets are blue" type
    poem

I want something deep

The feelings in the pit of your gut type of deep

The R-E-A-L in you

That can create the innate pulsations within me

You know it's hard for me to articulate my situation

Because I'm constantly contemplating how your manipulation
    of my feelings for you fall on deaf ears,

And it appears to me that you're not hearing me, so I'm gonna
    say it again,

Write me a poem!

So I can see what you can offer me through your words

And not your "dictionary" because

The way to my heart is not between my legs but between the
    whispers of sound your voice makes entering my mind

That's the type of stimulation I need

Let your *words* stroke me, let 'em evoke every feeling
    you're feeling,

Let your emotions recite to me, enticing me, inviting me into
    your world

So I can communicate with you through what you write…

In a poem

Beyond

180°

The young black boy lived a labeled life
Under yesterday's dreams,
Crafting jokes behind
Reality
The young black boy laughed and cried
Along his unmarked path
Helen Keller'd to his inner light
Dragging dreams inside loose jeans
And hardened eyes
I cry
This young black boy didn't know his worth,
Accepting pittance for pick-pocketed fantasies
And
Just as the breeze lifts an abandoned leaf
Into its highs,
It leaves it to drift back down into its emptiness
But, as the years have gone by,
My, have you transformed, young black boy
Just as the night blankets its days
You grew from your cocoon
And fueled hurt through art,
Lowering your fences
Through the beat of your heart
Through you, young black *man*,

Your story lives
And waits each day
For you to belt out
From the pit of your gut
To the ends of the skies
Until they cry out, "Surrender!"
Because they're full

Actionnairess

I am an actionnairess,

And I say this

With my head held high

And a pep in my step

Because I walk the talk

I am the verb you stalk

I don't need lights, cameras…just actions

My words have depth,

But my actions speak deeper

I am an actionnairess

'Cause taking action's so much sweeter

Anxiety

When in an anxious state,
the heart beats faster to feed the fears;
senseless thoughts produce senseless tears;
our inner voice is silenced by external mirrors—
daunting façades won't let you be.

When in an anxious state,
your pivotal achievements don't amaze
mere seconds feel like endless days;
they think this feeling is just a phase—
drifting away in search of Free.

When in an anxious state,
actions are frozen through mental deceit
Fear births acceptance of eternal defeat;
secured darkness is where your eyes retreat—
Dreams never swim with Certainty.

A User's Guide

Never announce you'll be more successful
Than those you know
Because they'll smell your arrogance and
Your true colors will show

Don't congratulate your peers
With a self-gaining opp in mind;
They'll sense your insincerity and
Leave your using [bleep] behind

Never say you'll look down from your big office
To wave at 'lil ol' me
And then come to me for a handout,
As if anything comes free

Once a user has tainted a relationship,
It is difficult to keep them
Around, so the only option is to
Kindly bless and release them

Book in Me

I've been pregnant for twenty years
Every morning, I've been sick
Of throwing up high hopes,
Heaving lost dreams
My feet are killing me
Defeat is swelling

I've been covering up my baby bump for twenty years
Wearing clothes that never fit right,
All to hide the growth within
Ignoring her kicks to be free

My water broke after twenty years,
And I was finally on Destiny's delivery table
With a few pushes and a couple pulls,
Out came my baby
I had a book in me,
And she's ready for the world to see

Change

Seasons alter leaves' complexion,
Caterpillars undergo a new formation.
Birds fly to a warmer location,
And snakes experience skin renovation.
Now this—this is change. And change is good.

Infancy to adulthood yields physical maturation,
Shackled souls seek divine elevation.
Switch lanes to reach your purpose-filled destination,
And become a "new" you—an immaculate revelation.
Now this—this is change. And change is good.

Clarity

I can't quite see through the fog,

But I'll keep walking

I don't know how deep the sea is,

But I'll keep swimming

I can't hear through the noise around me,

But I'll just listen

For the faint cue of clarity

I'd otherwise be missing

Deceit

When you lure me, masked

Into rooms of opulence,

Handing me, as an addict a needle

Corporate narcotics

Packaged in programmed rules

Hidden deceit

And blurred lines

Of a life not mine

I retreat

Detached

My parched eyes yearn

To connect to

The tender channels

Of a full heart

So that each pump pushes

The clear, salty truth,

Proving I'm no longer disconnected

Dreams

Let your eyes kiss its lids
and fall into blacks of nothingness
Awakening in mystic streams
of consciousness—
the insatiable desire to dream.

Look around with heightened senses
Dance with colors fixed in time
Spread your wings to soar with eagles
Until you're forced to go home
and live.

Empath

There is a bright-eyed girl
Sitting in Life's center,
Panning the world from left to right
As does a fan in an open room
People pass while nature's still
She inhales their worlds into her bright eyes,
And through her fingertips relinquishes their pain,
But from her trembling lips escape cries,
For their worldly woes have left her chained
And slightly dimmed

Four Elements

There are four elements of womanhood:
Earth, Water, Air, and Fire
Many claim to know the meaning of *woman*,
But through their acts does truth transpire

Does she walk barefoot through life's soils
Unmasked, natural, and pure?
Are her soles stained with humility
And poised with subtle demure?

Can you get lost in her sea of thoughts?
Does she take you for a ride
Into her depth and vastness?
Are you drenched by her tides?

Have you ever flown alongside her
And touched her limitless skies?
Soaring anywhere the wind blows,
Seeing dreams spoken through her eyes?

Do you feel the heat of her passion
Through her works and her tongue?
Do you ever get the feeling
That her destiny has just begun?

She is woman, she is woman
She is a true woman's desire
To embody the four elements of
Earth, Water, Air, and Fire

Hen Pen

Lord,

Please don't let me get sucked into a Hen Pen

Cluck, cluck-clucking with my fellow hens

How I deserve a man

How my feathers ain't attracting men

Lord,

I'd be enclosed in a cage of complaining hens,

Independent hens,

Desperate hens,

Negative hens,

Successful hens,

Lonely hens, and

Bitter hens

Oh, Dear Lord,

Please keep me away from those Hen Pens,

Where they brag about and list the assets they've laid

But are bitter when they never hatch

There's no consoling these hens, Lord!

They'll depress you even when you have a man!

Lord,

I pray for security and happiness,

Regardless of my status

'Cause I'll be damned if I start cluck-clucking at a Hen Pen

Hot Yoga

Stillness bounces freely

Between the inner pockets of self

When pregnant pores burst salty beads

In the sweltering 105 heat.

When contorted poses challenge balance

And focus, despite the turbulence

Where limbs and spirits

Swift through rapid movement,

Breathing to the beat.

Breaths of possibilities

Leave toxic puddles behind

As one tracks wet footsteps

To the serenity awaiting outside—

Namasté.

Human Hamster

Spin, spin, spin, little hamster
On that productivity wheel

Turn, turn, turn those spokes
Until your heels you cannot feel

Speak, speak, speak, little hamster
Just don't outshine me

Dim, dim, dim your light
'Cause only I can set you free

No, no, no, little hamster!
You can't leave your cage

Yes, yes, yes I can
It's time for *me* to take center stage

In a Moment in Time

Seasons change and moods swing

Dividing two worlds made one back into two

Your sun sets on my rising sun

I seek warmth when you're in need of shade

Holding hands with a familiar stranger

Brings a cacophony of thoughts in a moment of silence

Even our moments of silence have changed

In a moment in time

Intellectual Stimulation

Seek elevation

Slip inside your mind's stillness,

And bring words to life.

Lost

I don't know what He wants from me
Or where my purpose lies
It seems like everywhere I turn,
Uncertainty blurs my eyes

I don't know what to make of
What's presented at my feet
For all I know, it could be a false gift
With hopes packaged in deceit

I don't know what to do with myself
I'm so lost and confused
If only He could brighten my path,
So I can leave this place rescued

Masseuse

I lay on the operating table

Bare-skinned and open

Awaiting him

to take my body like dough and

Knead the knots,

Uncoiling fixed memories

Scalpel-like fingertips

Slice through scarred tissue,

Taking years of

Lumps and bumps that once crippled me

and vaporizing the pain through my pores—

Revealing the limberness

of a once tensioned soul

Metamorphosis

My past is where it should be,
Tucked away in a caterpillar's dreams
But it made me who I am
And everything I am to be.
While I snuggle into my humble home
Submerged in summoned thought,
I accept a part of me has to die
For another to be born.

I wake with second wind;
A metamorphosis of me
An evolution of me that
Unlocked what set me free.

Now, she can fan the skies
With her bold, patterned sheets
Unafraid to expand
And unravel what's beneath
But while the old may tug relentlessly
On the hope of present tense,
No other has control
But her; she will *fly* on
With no regrets.

No Other

When I hear others talk about their grandmothers,
There is no doubt in my mind that
No other can compare to you

There are men and women nearly twenty years your junior
With more prune to their skin,
Less sass in their walk
Cannot run a comb through their hair
And murmur when they talk
No other can compare to you

Who can say they've outlived their husband and friends
And stuck through hardships 'til the very end?
Most minds your age have lost their battle,
But you, you're a warrior who will never crumble
No other can compare to you

Behind those eyes lie years of wisdom
That pour through your lips to those who listen
Even through bodily pains you awake
To lift your hands up in praise to thank
The Lord for each and every breath you take
No other can compare to you

Post Grad Bluez

Where'd my money go?
Oh, yeah—on payday, she left
me for Sallie Mae.

Purging

Some labeled ill
Have mastered the art of releasing
To remove physical elements through
Visceral habits until the soul is at peace

But what was meant to abort
Leaves pieces that seep into its mental cavities
Frail walls can no longer support
The dichotomy of life and self

Inner banshees wail
While outer shells conceive contentment
Heart seeks a cure
But the mind just wants fulfillment

Rain

The sky cries

while trees tremble.

Detached leaves dance

with howling winds.

Birds draw near

to the one who stares,

to the one with fingers pressed

against her window's pain.

Seclusive Destruction

The slow demise of self is
Permanent seclusion
Back thrown out countless times from
Harboring scars and
Building invisible bars,
Ceasing all ties from both good and bad

Dressing Aloneness as
Self-Indulgence
Self-Programming the sense of
Productivity

From the world she
Hides cries
Behind yearning eyes, yet
She continues to destroy
Any seed from growing

Stallion

Majestic

Is your presence; it's captivating, honorable, and true.

This is what I'm drawn to—

The strength of a million men encased in a stare

And a regal strut whom no other can compare

Is it 'cause your skin's touch turns my life to gold,

Or that you share with me what your heart feared to unfold?

Is it your calmness in a world full of rage,

Or that you unlatched the hook to free me from my mental cage?

I don't know why I'm hooked

Like a moth to a flame

I don't know the reasons why, but all I ask is,

Will you be my stallion?

From your lips whisper, everything's okay.

Will you be my stallion?

Take my hand in yours, and let's ride away.

Calming

Is the sound of your mahogany melodies that make me

Foresee the universe, so that we can be

Free to believe in you and me,

Where we conceive visions, and now I see

I know why I'm hooked
Like a moth to a flame
I know the reasons why, and so I ask,

Will you be my stallion?
From your lips whisper, everything's okay.
Will you be my stallion?
Take my hand in yours, and let's ride away.

The Budding Rose

Closed doors clamped shut

by a padlocked life

to protect against forced entry

and trial-and-error woes.

But, only time does wait

for the inhale,

the exhale,

and the bloom of the budding rose.

The Storm

The clouds are crying on a mourning Monday,

Slipping tears from its hidden pockets,

Puncturing the earth's stillness

Winds howl at the crackling skies

Until each cloud's water breaks and bursts

Into its emotionally wet rage

The storm has come

It has come to free all those who've already been drenched

To My Son Not Yet Conceived

Before I make a home

For this burrowing seed

Within my blanketed walls of motherhood,

I make this wish for my little one,

To my son not yet conceived

I pray he walks along roads less taken

With pride, strength, and humility

That he goes where few others have gone

And raise from the dead, Chivalry

May his ego not grow too large

And link "I'm sorry" to defeat

That he'll assume his position at all times

And not cowardly take the backseat

To my son, not yet conceived,

I'll watch you grow from boy to man,

Embodying the wish I made way back when,

To live the title so many claim,

But few uphold its legacy

Trapped Until Freed

The trapped woman bleeds

through her ink-filled pen,

waiting for the chance

to release again,

and her words speak volumes

to those who receive it,

for this trapped woman

writes until she's freed

Truth

I stay slow and steady to win the race

Humble, while I keep the pace

Positive during roadblocks I face

To remind me of God's saving grace

'Cause without Him, I won't reach that place

Vicarious Girl

She exchanges emptiness for a character's tale
Ditches her host to transmit through them,
Leaving the tears in her host
To flee to temporary fulfillment because

She's a vicarious girl,
Vicariously living through another's vivid world,
Searching for a world that she loves the most,
Waiting for the next opportunity to leave her host

She replaces her life's deficiencies
For their life's proficiencies
Temporarily fulfilled
Until sucked back into her host's encasings

She's a vicarious girl,
Vicariously living through another's vivid world,
Searching for a world that she loves the most,
Waiting for the next opportunity to leave her host

Voice

The ones who speak least have the biggest voice
Deep-sea diving into inner thoughts,
Swimming through waters far past human survival
Into deep dark black pockets of mind
Where stillness speaks,
And they come back to the surface to share
Their voice

The ones who speak least have the biggest voice
It does not matter the mode they so choose
Through at least one of the five senses,
The message will reach
So others may tune into the eclectic symphonies of
Their voice

Who Am I? (A Lady's Anthem)

Who am I?
I'm a woman. A woman, am I? I *am*.

I am the Lord's Proverbs 31 woman
With strength like Alicia Keys's superwoman
Style like Kimora Lee's JustFab woman
I am Xena's warrior princess woman
I am

Who am I?

I am an esoteric essence of elegance woman
A mogul of immortal magnificence woman
A smooth, steady, and sophisticated woman
I am a beautiful, brave, and brilliant woman
I am.

Who am I?

I am the neck that controls the "head" woman
Aphrodite's true meaning of love woman
Aromatic like Jamaican spices woman
I am Maya Angelou's phenomenal woman
I am.

Now, who am I?

I'm a woman. A woman, am I? I *am*.

Short Stories

A Man of Few Words

It was the summer of 2004 when my mother, sister, and I visited my maternal grandfather in Jamaica. I knew our visit wouldn't end happily. My grandfather had stomach cancer, the result of his former heavy-drinking pastime. The cancer was so far advanced that not much could be done to reverse the tempest causing him to regurgitate life. Because he was given a few months to live, we came to say our last goodbyes.

    My grandparents have a veranda in front of their house, and as we pulled up the driveway, the first person I saw was him—Grandpa. He was sitting in his favorite spot, with his foot propped up on the railing. I hadn't seen him in about six years, and when I looked up at him on that veranda, I was searching for an ounce of excitement or happiness to see us. Instead, I found nothing in his eyes but a cold, blank stare.

    "Hi, Grandpa," I greeted him, still eager to get an emotion.

    He looked up at me and simply said, "Hi," and turned his head away to the distance. I could never figure out what he was thinking, or what it was about the space that kept him still. I waited for a minute before I put my bags in the house and stared at him. I can't even tell you what I was waiting for; I just looked at him looking at the world. I could see the sickness taking a toll on his body. He was never a big man, but when he looked into my eyes, his face was gaunt with his skin stretched thinly across his bones.

We spent a week in Jamaica, and the whole time I was there, I made an effort to get Grandpa to talk. I would come out on the veranda and share stories about school and my interests, and all he would say was, "Mmm-hmm." No eye contact, just a simple "mmm-hmm" to let me know he was somewhat present in the conversation. His stare never lost focus on space.

I was not used to the humid weather, so most of the time, I was dabbing my face and marinating in my own perspiration. But, every day, Grandpa sat outside in his same spot and would only come in to eat or when night blanketed the skies. I still didn't want to give up trying.

The next morning, I looked out the window to see Grandpa's back to me, with his hand propped up on his right cheek. I didn't want to leave here, or for him to leave *here* before I got him to open up. So, I got up, made some mint tea, and brought it out to him. He took the mug from me and simply said, "Thank you, ma'am."

Okay, strike two, I thought. I knew there had to be *something* that sparked his interest. I thought for a while, and then I went to my suitcase and took out a box of dominoes.

"You want to play, Grandpa?"

This time, he looked up at me and smiled—an irregular phenomenon. We played all day under the warm Caribbean rays. I can't describe how I felt when I played with him. He still didn't say much, but for that moment, we were doing something that brought him joy. I felt so much energy ping-ponging between Grandpa and me. We were bonding.

I don't know why I couldn't cry when my grandfather died, but what I am certain of is that I learned a lesson. I learned the power of communicating through action over words. The nonverbal can connect what the verbal may overlook. I connected with Grandpa that day, and I wouldn't trade that moment for anything in the world.

A MINDful Testimony

The mind is the most powerful and weakest element of the body. So powerful that it covers up the battered pieces of a forgiving heart. So weak that it is blinded by the windows peering out to a world of fantasy. A weak mind, strait-jacketed by life's heartaches, is so easily drawn to a single touch—one move, one glance, a state of vulnerability that I am well accustomed to.

So strong is the force that keeps me in this state of mind. So deep am I in this state of mental anguish. The air is crisp and clear, and yet it pains me to inhale its freshness. Pent up aggression hardened a heart of gold and left me in a trance—a stifling existence to which I've always believed to have no escape.

I am living, and functioning among the living, but not quite alive. In this world, but not part of this world, walking the paths of life with a hollow soul in search of a peace of mind.

And all that changed when his titillating presence stood before me. A wisp of cocoa butter and cologne splashed against his chocolate skin calmed me. It warmed my cold heart and revived a lost voice. He exhaled, I inhaled; he inhaled, I exhaled. Each breath evolved into an enchanting exchange of energy. I was captivated, but not quite the victim because all the while, I slowly but surely absorbed every ounce of life out of him. And then I stood there like a blood-thirsty vampire with my eyes fixed on his.

"What's on your mind?" He whispered as I inhaled. Such a loaded question; my mind and heart impregnated with memories and heartache and yearning that it triggered the river behind my eyes to overflow and dampen my cheeks. He proceeded to cup my face with his palms, the only hand I've seen big enough to scoop away my bucket of tears. Like a leech, I gravitated toward his presence.

He was a catharsis of sorts, who could open the deepest darkest portals of my mind. I exhaled. I escaped through him; which sent my mind into temporary paralysis. I welcomed the feeling of an empty mind and effortless sentiment.

And when he is no longer present, I'm left in the same agonizing predicament. I feel so dead inside. I look into his brown eyes, and he embraces me. What a necropheliac he is, for when he is gone, I'm no more than a corpse, waiting for the next escape to be alive and free again. Until then, my soul is abandoned and left to float among the careless of winds, carrying it far, far away into the shadows of the abyss—waiting to inhale, and then exhale again.

A MINDful Testimony – The Aftermath

This time, when I exhaled, the walls of comfort came crumbling down. It pierced my heavy heart, cleared my mind, and ripped the blindfolds off my eyes. I can see now.

Whom I ran to for comfort paralyzed my everything to the point where I was an emotional vegetable clenching on to life support I did not need. I am no longer a walking corpse; I took my life back. No, *God* gave me my life back, and for that, I am forever indebted. There was a time when I was on my knees crying out, beseeching to human flesh that would only spit venom on my frail disposition. I do not know how I still have the gift of sight because that night, each tear that broke its way out of my eyes burned in my sockets more than the last, but not as much as the dichotomy of sorrow and rage burrowing in my heart. I can feel now.

I once looked to human flesh for life and was led to drink from a cup of mental poison. I then turned to *Him* for life and He brought His cup to my lips, and I drank from Him for the first time in a long time. I am enlightened now.

My heart beats stronger and louder than before, in sync with the mind I was blessed with. There will be no more mental anguish; I am no longer enslaved by flesh and engulfed with guilt. I am free. I can breathe now.

Love makes time pass, but time makes love pass. Give me time, and I will press on. I am no longer in search of a peace of mind—this piece has found peace. I can live now.

Stage Five

I cupped my palms to scoop up the ice cold water running from the faucet and submerged my face into it. I needed to wake up. With my tired eyes, I caught my reflection staring back at me; all the while chanting to myself in a zombie-like fashion, "I will not pull another all-nighter again. I will not pull another all-nighter again."

It was a typical day for me, being awakened by the sun's rays trying to poke their way through the chilling morning clouds. I made mental notes of what I had to do throughout the day: 1) email professor, 2) go to work, 3) plan out life, and so on, and so on. I did this for about ten minutes.

It was getting late, and although I had gotten up an hour and a half before my class started, I still managed to be pressed for time. I dumped my notebook and all its contents into my bag, scorched my tongue in an attempt to gulp down my tea, and bolted out the door.

The air was so crisp that it quenched my skin's thirst. There was a soft breeze that flirtatiously wrapped itself around each leaf clinging to some branches nearby; they began to dance. A stray cat stopped and stared at me with his eyes fixed on mine. Its eyes were yellow; it matched the hue of the sun, which was slowly creeping its way to the middle of the atmosphere. All the while, some birds too lazy to fly hopped around on the pavement, their fury round bellies devouring their tiny feet.

I took my eyes off the peaceful scenery—I can't remember why; there was something that distracted me. Without any hesitation, I proceeded to continue my journey to class. As I was walking, the wind picked up, causing the clouds to cover the sun's radiance. There was a chill in the wind, and in turn, it sent a chill down my spine. I turned the corner, and before I could react, a dark figure tackled me like a football player to his opponent. I could not breathe. And then, a sharp object came in contact with my side, deeply piercing the flesh that once held my figure together. I did not know whether the blood had crawled down my legs or I had wet myself; it didn't matter. All that mattered was getting away. I screamed, but the figure muffled my cries. A tear escaped my eye, rolled down my cheek, and weaved itself through the creases of his fingers still clutched around my mouth.

No one came. I was afraid for my life. He then released his hand over my mouth and migrated toward my neck; he was trying to choke me. My eyes bulged as he squeezed my neck tighter and tighter. I could not take it anymore. I started kicking and screaming, scratching and clawing and somehow got away. I ran. And as I ran, a bright light flickered in my face, completely blinding me. I shielded my eyes, and when I opened them again, I…

…woke up.

The Race for Success

It is our greatest desire to shape our experiences into a life of purpose—a purpose that conditions us to breathe, eat, drink, and live for competition. We want to *win*. We need to win. We must win, and so we will run vigorously in the race for success and trample over any and all to win. We watch our neighbors, measuring *our* achievements against *their* successes. Jealousy and uncertainty begin to manifest. They will work together to unleash Fear to blindfold our Intuition, freeing the Ego encaged.

It is our greatest defeat to feed the self-serving beast within. Our souls will ache for power, yearn for prestige, and live diligently for ourselves. We will continue to make self-serving withdrawals from the Bank of Life until she handcuffs us and flings our shallow spirits onto the road of stagnation. Is this you?

It is our greatest truth when we realize that it is not about *ourselves*, it is about God and what we do for others. It is about incorporating animalistic, symbiotic truths into our daily practices. It is not about racing with agility and speed, but racing with a slow and steady purpose—*His* purpose. And then, if we stay the course, we may drink from the cup that overflows with divine eternal blessings—the true essence of success in its most fruitful form.

Taking a Leap of Faith

I think I speak for every twenty-something when I say job searching is a nightmare. It is a full-time job looking for a full-time job, and never mind the actual interview with the hiring manager; you're lucky if you even get a call back for the preliminary phone screening.

When you apply for a job, your fate lies in someone else's hands, and that is agonizing to think about. Someone is dangling a big juicy bone over your head while they decide where to drop it. While they decide, you're left to salivate and wait.

Let's just say I've had my fair share of salivating. I have applied to many jobs in my field, went on several interviews, and had my interviewee spiel practically memorized. I was nearly a year out of grad school and still unable to land a permanent home. I was getting restless. I was tired of the nomad life, bouncing from temp job to temp job with no clear destination. My contract was going to end in less than two weeks, and I needed a resting place. Fast.

I was in better spirits when a recruiter called me one Wednesday afternoon to schedule an interview. I overlooked the fact that I didn't care too much for the industry, and the office was miles and miles away from my home. All I cared about was securing a place to stay for more than three months. Mentally pushing all negatives aside, I confirmed the interview time and date and prepared like usual.

Interview day came, and I hopped in my car and headed to the middle of nowhere. Several winding roads and a number of peaks and valleys later, I pulled up to a drab building sandwiched between droopy, desolate trees. I went inside the building; the interior mirrored its external—dull, cold, and uninviting. The lackluster vibe was too much for my creative spirit, and I already had a bad feeling about this place.

My intuition was right. My interview with the hiring manager started off great, but almost as if someone had taken control of his body, he started to reek of chauvinism. I don't know when the transition happened; all I remember is that when answering one of his behavioral-type questions, he smiled and responded with a, "Good girl. I like that answer."

'Good girl?!' Although my head was spinning, I kept my composure. Some may have seen that as a harmless accolade with no meaning behind it. But, for me, that bugged the heck out of me because he already established a "man versus girl," "alpha versus beta," "master-dangling-bone-over-dog" relationship without even knowing it. Furthermore, as the interview progressed, the nature of the job started moving away from college-educated professional and more toward personal assistant. I thought to myself, Okay, God, how many more warning signs are you going to flash at me? After the interview, I graciously left the building, slumped into my car, and allowed the disappointment to seep through my pores.

To my surprise, I received a call a few days later from another recruiter to schedule an interview. This employer was closer, and I didn't mind the industry. Immediately upon entering this hiring manager's office, I felt a connection with her. I was greeted with a genuine smile, and when we shook hands, it felt as if we had a sisterly bond.

"There will be another round of interviews, and I definitely want you to meet my peers," she said, smiling from ear to ear. I was elated.

But after a few days, my elation was replaced with anxiety.

I was on edge every day, waiting for the call from my preferred employer. I was driving to work on a Thursday morning when I received a call from a private number. Assuming it was a recruiter, I anxiously answered the phone.

"Hello?" I said before holding my breath.

"Hello, Jennifer? This is [Recruiter] from [company in the middle of nowhere]."

My heart sank. I tried to mask my disappointment with an upbeat greeting.

"Good morning, [Recruiter], how are you?"

"I'm great. I am calling because I have some good news for you. The manager was very impressed with your interview and would like to offer you the position."

I was dumbfounded. This man actually wants to hire *me*.

I knew I shouldn't turn down this job. It would be dumb of me to say no to this lady and put all my hopes into *one* employer who was yet to schedule the second round of interviews, much less hire me. What are the chances of that happening? Jobs are too hard to come by. Even though I didn't care for the work environment, boss, or location, it was a job. It was more than I was getting paid then. And, it was permanent.

My internal dialogue lasted about two seconds. After the quick pause, I let the recruiter know I was being sought after by other employers and requested an extension to accept the offer. She gave me until the next day to make my decision.

As soon as I got to work, I emailed my preferred employer to let her know my situation. I told her I was offered a position, but she was my preferred choice. I also included that I was willing to take the risk and turn down this employer and pray for a rewarding outcome.

The preferred employer replied a few minutes later to let me know their recruiter would be making arrangements for me to come in the following week. Without hesitation, I wrote an email to the recruiter from the middle of nowhere, denying their offer—the most risky and courageous thing I've done in my professional career.

I went on to the second phase of interviews and spent three hours speaking with three of the hiring manager's peers. I later left the building feeling confident, but still uncertain. Had I made a mistake? Was it pretentious of me to deny an offer to seek a nonguaranteed opportunity? My mind was racing during the week-and-a-half wait for her decision. In my anxiety, I emailed the recruiter for a status. She said she would have an answer for me before the end of the week, close of business. I was being tortured beyond belief.

At about 4:50 p.m. on a Friday afternoon, I received the call I'd been waiting for. My preferred employer offered me the position—it was in a desirable location, an even higher pay, and I liked my boss. I was all smiles the entire weekend.

I know many would think I was crazy for taking such a chance, especially in these tough economic times, and I probably was. But, when you have an inkling burning inside, act even when you're unsure of the outcome. Dr. Martin Luther King, Jr. said it best, "Faith is taking the first step even when you don't see the whole staircase." I have come to learn that sometimes you just have to pray, and take a big leap of faith.

The Power of Patience and Prayer

In early 2011, I stood between two roads, both leading to potential career paths. I had always aspired to study law; everything I did in undergrad was geared toward law school. My plan was to take a year off and study for the Law School Admissions Test (LSAT) to obtain a more competitive score. I went through the application process in 2009, but did not get into any schools for Fall 2010. This was when I first felt defeated because my plans were not going the way I had hoped. According to my personal timeline, I was set back by yet another year. My goal was to be completely done with school by the age of twenty-five.

There was still room for improvement. I didn't make smart decisions when applying to law schools the first time around because 1) I did not select a broad enough range of schools to apply to (I only applied to schools in California), 2) My personal statement didn't reflect *why* I wanted to go to law school, and 3) My LSAT score was still not where I wanted it to be.

The next time around, I got a tutor, visited law schools, and built up my legal contacts of law students, judges, and attorneys. I took the LSAT in December 2010, my fourth time taking the exam, and after all the studying, money, and preparation, I barely improved. Trying to be positive, I went ahead and sent in all my applications, hoping I'd get accepted in to at least *one* of the fifteen schools in which I applied.

Rejection letter after rejection letter, I felt even more discouraged and unsure of what my next step should be. I had nothing but negative emotions during this period. My fear was that I wouldn't get in anywhere, and I would not know what to do with my life. I looked at master's programs, but I couldn't find anything that fit my interests other than law. I am the type of person who strives for continuous improvement and progression. Seeing people on social media hitting milestones such as marriage, family, continued education, and home ownership frustrated me because in my eyes, I was stagnated. I was forced to stay at a job I was miserable at and uninterested in. Despite all that I had accomplished, I still felt like a failure. I felt as though I was in a quarter-life crisis and stuck in a rut where I was no longer a child, but not yet an established woman. Tired of being depressed and sad almost every day, I decided to seek help in finding my way in life.

I could not have started going to bible study at a more appropriate time. Pastor Karen had just started talking about our thought-life and how negative thoughts and emotions yield negative outcomes. With the help of the prayer sheets and weekly meetings, I started praying more; asking God if law was not meant for me, then please show me the path that was.

I started racking my brain to come up with an Option B. I asked a friend how she liked the master's program she recently completed at Azusa Pacific University. She said she loved it and encouraged me to apply. I did some research on the program and applied while I waited for the law school decision letters.

Six days after applying to APU's Business Management program, I got a call from the enrollment counselor that I was accepted. Although I was happy that I finally had school security, I could not help the feeling of ambivalence bubbling in my spirit. I spent so much time, money, sweat, and tears to obtain a legal education, and to just drop it and do something else? But, after comparing the two routes, I saw that the master's program was a much better fit for me financially because I wouldn't be in as much debt, I could still meet my goal of finishing at twenty-five, and the career options available fell in line with my character and skills, probably even better than if I were to get a law degree.

Now that I look back, all the complaining I did was unnecessary. It was actually advantageous that I stayed at a job I didn't care for because I acquired news skills that would help me on my new path. This was a hard journey for me, but I have come to realize that everything will fall in place if you sit back and let God control. Although I am still working on my patience and allowing Him to take the reins, I know that in life, even when we try to predetermine our paths, there may be something unexpected that could change our course. I'm just happy that I trusted and believed He had a plan for me.

From Me to You

Dear Reader,

Thank you for accompanying me through my journey, my channeled energy. If you were moved by anything in this book, please share your thoughts on Instagram by using the #MyChanneledEnergy hashtag. Everyone has a story, but only few give voice to what's within. Be the few who do.

                                                        Blessings,
                                                        Jennifer

P.S. Please connect with me on Instagram or Twitter: @JenniferDVassel. I'd love to hear from you.

Appendix

"Sealed With a Kiss" Sources

Line 1: D.H. Lawrence: "Lightning"
Line 2: Anne Sexton: "After Auschwitz"
Line 3: D.H. Lawrence: "Lightning"
Line 4: Edgar Allen Poe: "Dream-Land"

Line 5: Michael Jackson: "Man in the Mirror"
Line 6: Tupac Shakur: "And Tomorrow"
Line 7: E.E. Cummings: "I Carry Your Heart with Me"
Line 8: D.H. Lawrence: "Lightning"

Line 9/10: Bliss Carmen: "A Northern Vigil"
Line 11: Bliss Carmen: "The World Voice"
Line 12: Tupac Shakur: "And Tomorrow"

Line 13: D.H. Lawrence: "Lightning"
Line 14: William Wordsworth: "Composed Upon Westminster Bridge, September 3, 1802"
Line 15: William Shakespeare: "Sonnet 18"
Line 16: Anne Sexton: "After Auschwitz"

Line 17: Jennifer D. Vassel
Line 18: W.B. Yeats: "A Dialogue of Self and Soul"
Line 19: Margaret Avison: "The Dumbfounding"
Line 20: Jennifer D. Vassel

Line 21: Emily Dickinson: "There Is Another Sky"
Line 22: William Shakespeare: "Sonnet 30"
Line 23: Edgar Allen Poe: "A Dream Within a Dream"
Line 24: John Donne: "The Canonization"